This book was made possible through
the generous assistance of

John Hancock

U S A

36 USC 380

OFFICIAL LIFE INSURANCE SPONSOR
1994/1996 U.S. OLYMPIC TEAMS

NORWAY

WELCOME TO THE 1994 OLYMPIC WINTER GAMES

By Robert Wulf

Photography By John Connell

Lillehammer'94

Page 1: A lone hiker stands atop Pulpit Rock, in southwestern Norway's Lysefjord, after a two hour climb. Over the edge is a vertical drop of more than 1,900 feet into water equally as deep.

Pages 2-3: A shaft of sunlight illuminates a tiny fishing hamlet off the southern tip of the Lofoten Islands in Northern Norway. Winter winds blow fiercely enough to require that structures be tethered to rock foundations with half-inch steel cables.

Dedicated to Johan Jorgen Holst and Mona Juul

Library of Congress Number:
Catalog Card Number: 93-94280

ISBN-1-883954-00-2

Printed in Hong Kong by Everbest Printing Company
through AsiaPrint/Everbest USA

Contents

———

Norway is a land virtually untouched. Despite its ancient Viking history—a millennium of struggle for independence as a free state—Norway is the cleanest, freshest and most natural nation in all of Europe. The Norwegians, full of pride and tradition, have assumed the role of Mother Nature's custodians. Today, the sea remains deep blue, the virgin snow still safe from the pollutants of industry. The land is truly unspoiled by man. This may be explained by Norway's comparatively spare population, despite its considerable geographic size.

Norway's turbulent past may also explain the country's relatively youthful demeanor. This magnificent territory was founded in the 11th Century, but was little more than a prize batted back and forth between the Swedes and the Danes for hundreds of years. The country Norwegians know today dates back as recently as 1814, when Norway finally won her unequivocal independence from Denmark, signed a new constitution, and proclaimed their king.

Norwegians are a society of people with a long history of tradition and culture. In some mysterious way they have managed to harness the relentless anger of the north sea and achieve the affluence of an industrialized nation without disrupting the simple way of life. A proud yet unpretentious lot, the Norwegians welcome visitors and invite them to enjoy their country and to have a first hand look at nature in its purest form.

This book seeks to paint a vivid portrait of the rich and varied drama of Norway. It pays very special tribute to the 1994 Olympic Winter Games, and Norway—specifically Lillehammer—is no stranger to the events. Winter sports—many of them born here—are as integral to Norway's culture as any architectural landmark, folk dance, or fjord to be found here. And no less dramatic in impact.

Welcome!

Oslo is a hospitable city of nearly 500,000 people located at the gateway of the Oslo fjord. The capital city rests on the low flat end of this fjord, allowing large ships easy access to the port of call. Unlike the over-urbanized existence of some Western European countries, here is a modern city surrounded by emanate beauty, with nature at its very doorstep.

Oslo is a city of contrasting architecture. There are no sweeping boulevards or imposing buildings competing for individual recognition, yet there is a mixture of old and new. Somehow, the haphazard arrangement of the streets flavors the air with a certain charm. The city is the tenth largest in the world geographically, but this statistic is nothing more than political convenience. Oslo is small and by no means does it compare to Stockholm and Copenhagen, let alone London, Paris or Rome. Oslo is not diminished by this; indeed, her charm is only enhanced by the comparison.

Much of little Oslo began its significant cultural and archi-

Left: Inclement weather in Oslo does not interfere with one of the most efficient public transportation systems in the world.

Above: Oslo was already 900 years old when these twin towers at City Hall were erected in 1950.

Previous pages 8-9: September in Fagernes.

Previous pages 10-11: Very little of Norway's land is suitable for farming. But here along the Hardangerfjord, warm waters from the Gulf Stream and long hours of sunshine during the growing season make for a prosperous fruit industry.

tectural ascent in history after Norway's 1814 independence. Karl Johans Gate was started in 1818 and completed in 1848, and it remains Oslo's main thoroughfare today. The city's principal buildings date from the mid-19th Century. The most significant architecture dating from this time can be viewed together along one particular mile-long stretch of Karl Johans Gate: the Royal Palace, constructed in the early to mid 1800s; the handsome Neoclassic facade of the University of Oslo, built from 1811; and the National Theater, the most representational of the late 19th Century. It's one of the focal points of the capital's cultural pride. Appropriately, statues of Norway's most distinguished pens, Henrik Ibsen and Bjornstjerne Bjornson, flank the National Theater's entrance. The theater has been newly renovated after a backstage fire in 1982 closed its main stage and auditorium.

Today, the National Theater is one of the most famous theaters in Western Europe. People from all over the world travel to Oslo to see classical performances of the works of Ibsen, Shakespeare, Chekhov, Brecht and many others. Directly across the street from the National Theater is the Theatercafe, an integral part of the the-

Left: A stonefaced Henrik Ibsen stands tall in front of the National Theater. The famous playwright, whose "Peer Gynt" has been performed here over 700 times, was shrewd enough to be one of the first stockholders in the National Theater Ltd. after it opened in 1899.

Above: Inside, the original rococo auditorium survived a fire that destroyed the main stage in 1982.

*Above: Directly across from the National
Theater stands the Hotel Continental
and Theatercafe, where many of Oslo's
distinguished faces can be seen.*

*Right: Karl Johans Gate, Oslo's main
thoroughfare, gets all decked out for May
17th, Norway's Constitution Day.*

Following pages 18-19: Spring in Oslo.

ater experience here. Located on the main floor of the completely restored Hotel Continental, the cafe offers fine continental cuisine and wines 'till the wee hours of the morning.

Directly south of the National Theater stands Norway's most visible reminder of its rocky history of occupation and struggle: the Akershus Fortress, overlooking the port of Oslo. Since the Middle Ages, Norway has been an insignificant player on the European stage. Norway served as land prize to be awarded back and forth between raging neighbors Denmark and Sweden, and Norway fell randomly under the rule of each. Oslo's Akershus Fortress was the strategic point defending incoming attackers by sea.

In 1310 Duke Erik of Sweden attacked and successfully besieged the Akershus just 10 years after it had been completed. Christian II of Denmark regained possession in 1531-2, and again Akershus was taken by the Swedes in 1537 and 1716.

The long, low bulk of the fortress was built by King Haakon V in the early 14th Century. It is an impressive building of massive spires and jutting roofs. From 1940-45, Akershus served as the Nazi Occupation headquarters for Oslo. It is only fitting today that the fortress houses the Resistance Museum which graphically charts the Nazi Occupation and the heroic efforts of Norway's resistance.

From the east wall of the Akershus across the harbor, the contrast of modern urban living spreads out in stark contrast to this 14th-century castle. It is the newest addition to the mixture of archi-

tecture in Oslo. The waterside Aker Brygge is a shopping and leisure center consisting of a myriad of small cafes, ethnic restaurants, both indoor and outdoor, as well as several theaters, office buildings and apartment dwellings.

On the outskirts of Oslo proper is Vigeland Park and Sculpture Garden. Perhaps the most striking sight in all of Oslo can be found here. Sculptor Gustav Vigeland created a dramatic 60-foot-high monolith carved from a single block of stone and weighing 200 tons. Vigeland also designed the park; in addition to the monolith, Vigeland contributed nearly 200 sculptures which took him 40 years to complete. Vigeland's central theme portrays the cycle of life. The main corridor leading up to the monolith is lined with bronze sculptures which mark the progress of man beginning with birth, then childhood, adolescence, maturity, old age and death. In the foreground of the monolith stands a massive fountain. It is supported by six monumental figures symbolizing man's burden. Surrounding gardens flourish with brilliant roses and tulips. The remaining landscape consists of contoured rolling hills of finely groomed grass and large trees indigenous to the region. Further evidence of Vigeland's prolific work can be seen at the Vigeland Museum. The museum contains 1,650 sculptures, 12,000 sketches and 3,700 wood carvings. The sig-

Left: A steep cobblestone path leads to the burial ground of several Norwegian kings at Akershus Castle.

Above: This young man stands watch over what is today the Resistance Museum at Akershus.

Below: Solid construction techniques have kept Akershus in one piece for almost 700 years.

nificance of Vigeland's work acclaims him as one of the great sculptors in Norwegian history.

In order to grasp the diverse contrast of the environmental elements of Oslo, one must not overlook the Holmenkollen. In Norway, where skiing was invented 4,000 years ago, a pictograph carved into a rock is the world's first known illustration of a person skiing.

Ever since, sports have been an intrinsic part of this Nordic country's culture —as much a part of its culture as music, dance and nature. Indeed, to many Norwegians, Holmenkollen's significance is regarded as a symbol of Norway. The principal attraction for visitors is the ski jump itself, where an elevator ride to the top of the jump reveals the death-defying challenge of this perilous sport. About 200 yards below the jump is the Holmenkollen Park Hotel. Built in 1892, the hotel was designed in the ancient dragon style and constructed almost entirely of wood. Inside, the main hall is lined in wooden panels carved with scenes from the saga of Sigurd the Dragon Killer from the collection of the wood carver John Borgersen. In the winter flaming torches in the snow light the roads all through the Holmenkollen Park. Horse-drawn sleighs are the most exciting way to experience the magic of a Norwegian winter night.

Much can be said about Oslo, but nothing says it better than Constitution Day, where school children march behind brass bands and banners as they wind their way along Karl Johans Gate before climbing the hill to the Royal Palace to greet the King and Queen.

Today, though still somewhat of a toy town, Oslo remains a harmonious and civilized place that has certainly put its troubled history behind it.

Above: Modern architecture sprouts from what was until recently a shipbuilding district, at Aker Brygge.

Following pages 26-27: Akershus steals the spotlight after dark.

Right: Youngsters take a break from a field trip with a game of ring-around-the-Royal-Palace.

26

Left and above: The work of the prolific sculptor Gustav Vigeland, who master-planned the 650-acre park that bears his name.

Following pages: Water sheets off a towering bronze sculpture at the very center of Vigeland.

Left and above: Subtleties go out the window as nature's vibrant color schemes take over this bed of tulips near Aker Brygge.

Left and right: The Holmenkollen Park Hotel sits high above Oslo, adjacent to the ski jump erected in 1952 for Norway's first Olympic Games. Opened in 1892, the hotel has recently been developed into a state-of-the-art conference center.

Following pages: Peace and quiet on the Hardangerfjord minutes before rainfall. In the background is one of 28 glaciers to be found in this region, which equates to about one glacier per 142 inhabitants.

*Above: Protected from the North Sea
by mountains that shoot straight from
the water, and influenced by the heat
of the Gulf Stream, the Lofoten
Islands are considerably warmer than
other places of the same latitude.*

*Right: Islanders can escape the
momentary confines of a small town
and partake in all manner of outdoor
activities, one of which is mountain
climbing.*

Left: Constitution Day: Everyone in Norway turns out for the May 17th celebration, and this little village on the southern tip of the Lofoten Islands is no exception.

Above: Stern faces are de rigueur here, Constitution Day or not. Life above the Arctic Circle has it's share of hardships, but on this day these brooding countenances are made worse by a celebration-induced lack of sleep the previous night.

Above: The 90 meter ski jump will funnel the world's finest ski-jumpers into the landing area in the center of an open-air amphitheatre during the 1994 Lillehammer Olympic Games. At the bottom of the hill is one of three ice rinks built for the games.

Following pages 44-45: From here and many other vantage points across Lake Mjosa, a good set of binoculars and a rooftop seat are all that's needed to witness the ski jumping competition.

N ORWAY'S LILLEHAMMER WILL embellish sports history forever as the host of the 1994 Olympic Winter Games. But to the people of this small Scandinavian town, history and winter sports are part of everyday life and have been for nearly 5,000 years. Skiing is considered Norway's national sport. Organized ski competition dates from 1843 in Tromso, but not as an Olympic event. However, both London in 1908 and Antwerp in 1920 already included winter sport events in their programs. In 1922 the International Olympic Committee decided to organize and combine Winter and Summer Olympic events on a trial basis. Thus, the first official Olympic Winter Games were held in Chamonix, France in 1924.

Located approximately 100 miles north of Oslo, Lillehammer is a quaint alpine village of 22,000 inhabitants. Storgata, or Main Street, runs through the center of town and is Norway's longest small town street. For pedestrians only, Storgata is lined with two-story wooden houses with saddled roofs and bay windows. These late 19th-century structures have since been converted to shops, restaurants and pubs, with the inherent charm of Storgata completely intact for visitors. The best-preserved traditional structures are currently being considered for architectural heritage protection.

A few blocks from Main Street, the 1895 Bank of Lillehammer building is a highlight of Norwegian culture and royal history. In 1991 the building was renovated to serve primarily as a facility for Norwegian nobility during the Olympic Games. Numerous activities will be held during the games for royal and honored guests of the King and Queen. The royal family will host performances of Norwegian folk music and dance in period costumes dating from the 15th

century. Norwegian cuisine and spirits will be prepared and served at formal dinners in the traditional style.

When The International Olympic Committee awarded Norway the bid to host the XVII Olympic Winter Games, Lillehammer became the focus of a national debate regarding the environmental impact from an event of such magnitude. Norwegian activists lobbied the country's legislators to allocate funds for a management group called Project Environment-Friendly Olympics. Its purpose: To protect Mother Nature from the short-sightedness of land developers and politicians. The exhaustive efforts of Project Environment's task force—upholding the ethics of site planning, energy efficiency, construction materials, re-cycling and post-Games usage of facilities—has given Lillehammer the new designation as host of the World's first "Green Games." Environmentalist concerns also prompted the Lillehammer Olympic Organizing Committee to insure that the planning and construction of all events would rest peacefully with nature. At the bobsled and luge track, a fine was imposed for cutting trees—up to $10,000 each. The track design subsequently snakes through the trees and along the natural contours of the topography, and few trees were cut.

The ice hockey rink in nearby Gjovik is built in a cavern, leaving no significant signs of its existence from the exterior. The biathlon, combining cross-country and rifle events, required a special bullet collection device which stops spent lead from sinking into the soil and contaminating the ground water. Master planning an "environmentally correct" Olympic Games is no easy task. Adhering to Norwegian tradition, planners carefully plotted architectural designs which respond to the elements of the natural topography or reflect

Right: The bobsled/luge track carefully follows the contours of this hillside, and the entire facility blends almost seamlessly into the landscape.

an important remnant of ancient history. The ice rink in Lillehammer is oriented in such a way that its roof line is proportionately contoured to blend in with surrounding hillsides. The speed skating rink in Hamar resembles an overturned Viking ship. These three structures, along with the Olympic Village where athletes are housed during the Games, have the most significant impact to the environment.

In the heart of town other buildings have been constructed and renovated. The train station is completely restored, and the Molla Hotel is completely renovated with an all-glass rooftop bar and lounge which to the west overlooks the 90 meter ski jump and to the east Lake Mjosa. There are two new museums downtown, both related to Olympic history. Streets have been resurfaced and some new ones built; the rail system has been upgraded between Oslo and Lillehammer and other surrounding areas—all in the effort to accommodate the estimated 100,000 people a day expected to swarm the Olympic Village during this historic fortnight. And the cost for the country of Norway to stage this event: 700 million dollars.

Left: One of many examples of traditional architecture in downtown Lillehammer.

Above: Lillehammer's train station was renovated in anticipation of the '94 Olympic Games. Several thousand people a day are expected to arrive by rail during the Games.

Off the slopes, Lillehammer's best known attraction is the open-air Maihaugen Museum. Founded in 1887 by Anders Sandvig, Maihaugen is the inspiration of one man who wanted to preserve the old Gudbrandsdalen culture from being lost to future generations. The village of 130 authentic buildings tells a story of life in the Middle Ages. There are individual family dwellings, dry food storage houses, small structures to protect farm animals during winter storms, a schoolhouse, church, parsonage, and the village hall. In 1907 Sandvig expressed the purpose of his work in the following terms: "As I see Maihaugen, it is to be a collection of homes where one can almost meet the people who lived there, understand their way of life, their tastes, their work. But it is not merely a chance collection of individual homes that I intend to preserve from destruction and oblivion at Maihaugen. On the contrary, I shall provide a full-scale illustration of a village as a whole."

If Ibsen's famous character Peer Gynt had known of Sandvig's dream, perhaps he too would have experienced Maihaugen. Doubtless, this full-scale time capsule will have grown in historic stature by the close of Lillehammer's games.

Right: The Molla Hotel is a converted grain mill, and its uppermost level affords bar patrons sweeping views of Lillehammer.

Below: The hotel basement has been converted into a cozy, seven-level restaurant.

Left: The King and Queen of Norway will host many cultural and social events at this intimate performance theater (formerly the Bank of Lillehammer) during the course of the 1994 Olympic Winter Games.

Above: Royal guests will be comfortable in this beautifully crafted seating parlor adjacent to the theater.

53

Above: Students congregate at the steps of
the new Lillehammer Art Museum.

*Above: Lillehammer's pedestrian-only
Main Street will be covered in snow and
teeming with visitors during the Games.*

Southern Norway explodes with spring color.

Above: From January through April, arctic sea cod are drawn into the Vestfjord by the temperate waters of the Gulf Stream, and upwards of 3,000 fishermen go out to meet them each year. Once cleaned, the cod is hung from the tail to dry for months on wooden racks like these.

Left: Hanging cod indicates the end of fishing season, and small harbors like this one are mostly idle.

Above: Small fishing vessels surround an old slate-roofed boathouse near Bergen. A common roofing material in Norway, slate "shingles" can be found in huge piles behind virtually every farmhouse.

*Above: Late afternoon in Henningsvaer,
the Lofoten Islands' largest fishing village
and home of the Queen's favorite fish soup.*

BERGEN SEEMS FOREVER PERCHED
on the edge of adventure. Located on the Western shore of Norway,
Bergen is the threshold between the mountains and the sea. It is a
fascinating mixture of old and new, a city with a heart of its own. A
cusp between two of the most famous fjords in the world—the Songefjord
to the north and the Hardangerfjord to the south—Bergen is the gateway to Norway. The Hardangerfjord is the longest fjord in the world,
reaching inland from the North Sea more than a hundred miles. For
nearly a thousand years the sea and connecting fjords was the vital
link for fishing and trading vessels to the people of Bergen. Com-
merce was divided in 1909 when the rail system was completed from
Oslo to Bergen, adding strength to Oslo and weak-
ening Bergen. Today, much of Bergen's economic live-
lihood is centered upon the North Sea Oil Industry.

More than any other city in Norway, Bergen
is quintessential Old World Europe. Walking along
the wharf of old town at night, the dim glow of dis-
tant lights from across the shore tells a rich story of
romance and beauty. Founded by King Olav Kyrre
over 900 years ago, the city was Norway's capital and
the largest trade port in Scandinavia throughout the
Middle Ages. Ancient harborside dwellings which
still stand today are testament to the Hanseatic mer-
chant lifestyle. They are a living museum of tall, dark
wooden buildings with sharply pointed gables and
narrow alleyways running through to workshops and
courtyards behind. They stand in the lee of a fortress
called Bergenhus, once a royal residence and still the

*Below: Geraniums grace windowsills
everywhere in Bergen.*

*Right: One of Bergen's main
thoroughfares leads to the Funicular,
an eight-minute cable car ride to the
top of Mount Floyen.*

*Following pages 64-65: The view from
Mount Floyen. Bergen has been
referred to as the "Gateway to the
Fjords". It is Norway's second largest
city, and a huge draw for cruise ships
from all over the world.*

Above: Bryggen waterfront.

scene of royal banquets. The Bryggen is the most recognizable land-mark to visitors of Bergen, which today houses a variety of shops, offices, restaurants and night clubs. Adjacent to the Bryggen is the fish market and fruit stand where locals and visitors alike can find some of the freshest foods in the world.

Bergen's society prides itself on art, music, theater and education. The Bergen Municipal Art Gallery was opened in 1878 and houses a representative collection of Norwegian paintings from the 19th and 20th Centuries as well as a small collection of European paintings. J. C. Dahl, considered the father of Norwegian painting, is well represented here, as are Norway's romantic artists Hertervig, Tidemand, Gude and others. Naturalism and Neo-Romanticsm are displayed through the works of Christian Krohg, Erik Werenskjold and Harriet Backer. The present century is represented by Munch, Astrup, Turnold, Sorensen and Fjell. Foreign paintings include the works of Picasso and Braque. The Stenersen Collection, purchased by the city in 1971, boasts the works of Picasso, Miro, Leger, Toulouse-Lautrec, Kollwitz, Klee and Ernst. The Rasmus Meyer Collection

Above: A short subject is dressed for inclement weather in Bergen.

Left: It has been said that rain is a Bergen specialty; precipitation falls an average of 250 days a year here. But today is a day to take the kids out for a stroll.

includes the works of Dahl, Wold-Torne, Werenskiold, Munch and others.

Many famous people have come from Bergen such as Dahl and Christian Michelsen, who was Prime Minister in 1905. But unquestionably is the trio: Ole Bull; Ludvig Holberg, who lived much of his adult life in Copenhagen but always considered his home Bergen; and, most famous of all, Edvard Grieg.

Born in Bergen June 15, 1843 Edvard Grieg was a devoted composer, pianist and conductor of great music until his death in 1907. Today, 86 years later, he still enjoys an international reputation as a major classical composer. The composer of "Peer Gynt," Grieg toured Europe throughout his career, playing and conducting in some of the most prestigious concert halls and chambers. Part of his greatness as a composer was his ability to unite traditional Norwegian folk melodies with the fashionable European music of his time. He helped to strengthen the Norwegian national identity while bridging the culture of his country with that of the rest of Europe. As 1993 marks the 150th anniversary of Grieg's birth, the Norwegian Government, the Department of Foreign Affairs and the City of Bergen presented "Grieg-Jubileet 1993." The celebration traveled to the United States, Canada, Japan, Germany, France, the United Kingdom, Spain and Italy.

It could be said that Bergen is a city of romance and charm. Its rich ancient history is as colorful as any in the world. But when one peers across the harbor from Floyen, Bergen is undoubtedly the city of lights.

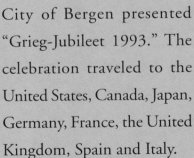

Above, below and right: The home of Norwegian composer Edvard Greig.

Above: Lace-framed windows let in Norway's local color.

Left: Farmhouse in Fagernes.

Above: Fiery tulips at dawn.

Left: Churches dot the Norwegian landscape.

Above: September in Ulvik.

DEEP FOREST, BROAD MOORS, sparkling tarns, foaming waterfalls, snow-clad peaks and rolling hill-sides best describe the Fagernes region. The hospitality of the people is a living, vibrant cultural tradition. It is a tranquil and spacious place, inviting reverie and silent fantasy. The spirit of adventure lurks everywhere. Many people refer to this area as a kingdom—with good reason. The Fagernes area embraces the unspoiled beauty of nature like no other. It is a treasure trove of unforgettable sights and sounds of mountains, lakes and wildlife. Children and adults alike can experience more in a Fagernes day than a visit to a thousand theme parks.

Fagerness earned its reputation as a kingdom for another reason: the King's Road, constructed to link Oslo with Bergen, passes through the Fagernes area, and still exists today. A journey along its now smooth paved road is a breath-taking experience. It is a timeless venture of beauty, history and tradition. Sites along the route date back to 700 A.D. The feeling of standing in a cemetery and reading tombstones from a thousand years ago chills the spine with an eerie melancholy. The varied beauty to be found along the route—the stillness of a majestic lake, the sun hitting a clearing in the trees, the

Left and below: Water, water, everywhere. Fagernes is a second home to many well-to-do Norwegians who might have both a city apartment and a mountain retreat.

painterly aspect of the country-side—must be experienced for its full impact. It cannot accurately be put into words.

To the south of Fagernes one can find a unique type of calm in the Tislei Valley. The Tisleia River is a dream come true for the angler, but for the quiet mountain lake lover, one must descend into the valley.

At the heart of this kingdom is the town of Fagernes itself. It is big enough to have paved streets and modern necessities, but is also small enough to get to know people from all over the world in one of many quaint restaurants and pubs.

Here, tradition still forms part of everyday life. Folk music, local cuisine and the traditional arts and crafts are practiced year round. People are attracted by the genuine, warm demeanor of the locals, the scenery, and the Strandefjord—where in the summer one can sail, windsurf and swim in the warmth of this pleasant climate.

Far from everyday life here is Vang, located northwest of Fagernes and nestled between Jotunheimen and the deep fjord of the west coast. Vang is an area of contrasts, with fertile valleys and rugged mountains. Kings, painters, poets, and others have arrived here, and finding the surroundings agreeable, decided to stay for awhile. Few other places contain such a fascinating mixture of scenery and culture. Heading towards Jotunheimen, the spirit of Ibsen's Peer Gynt is in the air....

Fagernes lies approximately 60 miles due west of Lillehammer. Like Oslo and other surrounding communities, Fagernes will provide a portion of the housing accommodations during the Olympic Games. With such broad visual and emotional brush strokes separating these regions, visitors would be hard-pressed to choose between them. Fortunately, transportation to and around Lillehammer has been given special attention, and there should be no reason for visitors to miss any of the history of Oslo, or the drama of Fagernes—while they aren't thrilling to the luge, screaming for their favorite skaters, or skipping a heartbeat over the fastest skier.

Left: Farms dot the rolling hills of Fagernes. Virtually all are small, self-supporting family farms, and long winters followed by short summers make for less-than-ideal agricultural conditions.

Previous pages 82-83: Groundcover glows during mid-September in the Valdres area, but the first winter snow will blend these colors into a dull gray overnight.

Above: This striking piece of modern Lofoten residential architecture also comes with a sizeable backyard.

Right: This old sawmill was in operation until 1945, and until recently was only accessible by boat. But the Norwegian government stepped in after the death of its last owner and decided to turn it into a museum. After a cost of five million dollars to bore a two-mile tunnel through solid granite for automobile access, reconstruction of the mill is under way.

Above: Detail of a dwelling-house in Maihaugen, an open-air folk museum near the Olympic Village in Lillehammer. The current King and Queen of Norway will be staying in a brand new "old-style" dwelling-house during the Games, handcrafted to their exacting specifications.

Left: Interior of Maihaugen's small church.

Top: One of three completely intact
Viking ships to be found in the Viking
Ship House in Oslo. This sturdy vessel
sailed the belligerent North Sea over
1,000 years ago.

Above: More evidence of Viking lore
can be found in Stavanger.

Right: Viking hieroglyphics, also in
Stavanger.

WHEREVER YOU GO IN NORTH-land, town or country, you are close to the loveliest, wildest and most contrasting surroundings conceivable. Its fascinating sites and natural phenomena have inspired such literary giants as Edgar Allan Poe and Jules Verne.

The Northland is a place where everything stands exactly where it was created. Traces of Early Man immortalize the Northland habitants. Symbols of everyday life represent man's existence as early as the Stone Age. Traces exist even today where Iron Age Man raised his turf huts, the grave sites of Viking chieftains and kings, the houses and churches of medieval clergy, and the mountains where the Lapps performed their sacrificial ceremonies. Norway stretches to the top

Below: Dog sledding is a favorite Norwegian winter pastime.

Left: The road to Vikten. Northern Norway's only glass blowing house is located here, and the proprieter is a tenth-generation Viking. Vikten is home to a tightly knit group of Norwegian citizens-against-MTV (and other media influences); television, radio and satellite dishes have been outlawed by public decree.

of the world—a tenuous link between north and south. At one point the land narrows to 6 kilometres separating Sweden from the sea.

But Northland is more than a buttress that keeps the Kingdom of Sweden from falling into the sea. It is a land of mountains, rich in minerals; of fjords rich in fish and mainland and islands rich in history and mystery. The Lofoten Islands string along the northwest coast of Norway, beginning at the outer perimeter of the Arctic Circle and extending north to the connecting islands of Vesteralen and continue to the far reaches of Norway.

Northland rests in the Arctic Circle—imaginary, yet so real it bounds the midnight sun of the Arctic summer and the sunless winters of the north. Despite the two months of darkness that occur here, scientists have calculated that the sunny nights and bright days, the moonlight, starlight and northern lights collectively give more light in the course of a year than one can experience at the equator.

The northern lights of *Aurora Borealis*, the flaming spectacle of the Arctic winter sky with its flickering and undulating move-

Above: A rare bolt of sunlight shimmers on the Vestfjord, between Bodo and Lofoten.

Left: A polar bear is on top of the world navigating the ice flows.

ment of vibrant yellows, greens, reds and violets fill the sky with mystery. So mysterious, powerful and alarming is the Aurora, that when it was observed in the more southerly skies, people took it as an omen of impending wars and disaster. This phenomenal sighting every year is one of the most overwhelming natural spectacles on Earth.

The Arctic Circle also marks the northernmost existence of several species of flowers and trees, blocked by Arctic climate and the Saltfjell mountains. Temperatures here are prohibitive to such temperate-loving trees as elm, ash and linden. And yet there are more than a million acres of productive forest, consisting of 45 percent conifers and the rest deciduous, mainly birch. Spruce can be found as far north as the foothills of the Saltfjell. The pine is the only conifer growing wild north of the Saltfjell.

Left: Reindeer graze nonchalantly. Moose and reindeer are likely to be found on any decent Norwegian restaurant's menu.

Following pages 96-97: Spring changes gradually to summer on the west coast of the Lofoten Islands.

Above: Christmas celebrations in the far north.

Right: A dark and cold winter's day in the northernmost regions.

This mountain range is also too intemperate for inhabitants of the snake persuasion—a fact which no Northlander finds regrettable. But the people appreciate and cherish the animals which do exist here: the reindeer, lynx, fox, marten, otter, beaver, sea eagle, golden eagle and many more.

The sea that laps the coast of Northland is the home to some of the finest edible fish in the world, and extending to seals and porpoises, sperm and bottlenose whales, killer whales and dolphins. For the price of an inexpensive fishing license, anyone can fish in more than 28,000 lakes, with a surface area of nearly 2,500 square miles.

The mystery of the Northland and the people who inhabit this most unusual region of the earth live with the uncontrollable elements of nature. Uncommonly so, it is one of the most beautiful and striking sites on earth.

Above: Moose country in Fagernes.

Above: Hamnoy, Lofoten Islands.

Left: Fagernes lights up at dawn.

Above: Arable land is scarce in Norway; red paint is not.

THROUGHOUT NORWAY CULTURE
and tradition are constitutional among her people. Perhaps the richest legacy of the Norwegian people is their love affair with the land and sea. A land rich with timber, minerals and stone, Norway and her inhabitants wisely made friends with one another long ago, and this symbiotic relationship remains in evidence today. A close look at early architecture tells us the builders were pragmatic with their approach to construction. The use of sod roofs is an ingenious discovery which is still used today in many parts of the world, including the United States. In the summertime, grassy roofs protect the moist soil from sun dehydration, thus cooling the interior of the house. Conversely, winter weather freezes the soil and serves as a natural insulator against the harsh northern storms. Elevated food storage houses were designed to increase air circulation from beneath the floor, adding shelf-life to grains and perishable food.

One of the most famous architecture statements in Norway is

Previous pages 106-107: Water power plant in Ardal.

Previous pages 108-109: Bygdoy folk museum detail. Sod roofs have been in use for hundreds of years, and are often utilized in new construction for their insulating properties and asthetic appeal.

Above: This dimly lit hut is typical of those built during the 18th-century in Norway. Dressed in traditional clothing, a young woman complements this folk museum interior.

Left: Bygdoy.

the Stave Church. The construction of this church incorporated a special corner-locking design technique which bonds log timber walls—much like a log cabin design. An oversized timber footing adds strength to the wall structure. This technique formed the basis of what is now known as post-and-beam construction. Structures from this period have very small window and door openings which improved overall structural integrity and diminished wind drafts during the winter season.

The virtue of this hand and earth relationship can also be seen in various types of arts and crafts. Most early tools were made of wood. These included farming, building, common utility items (such as water troughs), and household items—like mixing bowls, bread pans and tableware. Artisans carved mythological characters of the time from large blocks of pine. This movement inspired progressive-thinking artists to experiment with new materials. The discovery of iron—and more importantly the ability to shape and forge with heat—developed a new age of tools and weapons which improved farming and hunting skills.

Above: Many students find summer employment as museum guides.

Left: Norwegians collect old churches and put them into folk museums when possible. This church has been relocated to Maihaugen, near the Olympic Village in Lillehammer.

Above and below: Fine hand-blown crystal has been an integral part of Norwegian culture for more than 250 years.

Right: The Glassworks in Hadeland is a major tourist attraction for travelers who take the King's Road. Demonstrations are held every two hours at the Glassworks.

Much of the development of fine art and crafts began about 250 years ago in the Hadeland region, just north of Oslo. Glasswork and pottery was the main focus of most artists. The Hadeland Glassworks and Museum began in a barn in 1762. Today, the Glassworks is a massive facility of more than 25 buildings. The production facility welcomes the public to see molten glass hand-blown into beautiful works of art by resident artists. The original structure has since been converted to a restaurant and accommodates 400 guests.

Hadeland Glassworks is the second oldest facility in Norway and is one of the largest in Scandinavia. The Hadeland Glass Museum was built on site, commemorating 225 years of art glass. The oldest glassworks are on the lower level of the museum. Four free-standing glass cases display glasswork in chronological order from 1750-1920.

Of special interest are chandelier pieces from the middle 1700s. Many have been restored and some parts duplicated to exact perfection. There is a collection of bottles and other everyday products made during Hadeland's "Bottle" period, from 1760-1850. This 90-

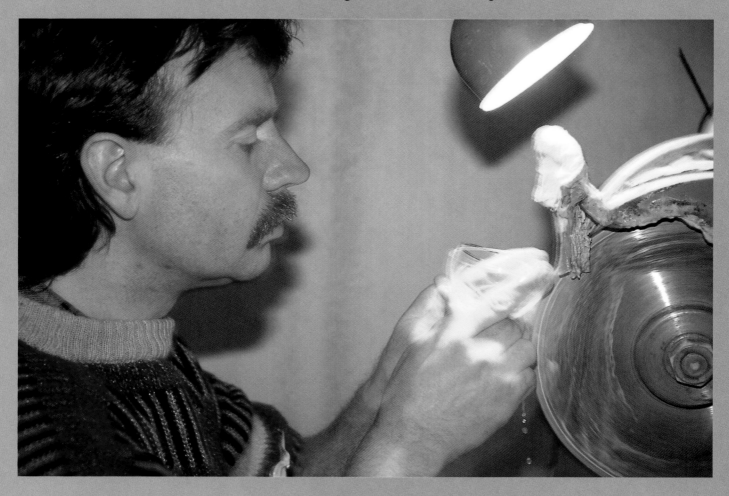

Above: Reindeer ranching in Northern Norway.

Left: Traditional dwelling of the north.

year period is characterized by a limited selection of work. At its height, Hadeland made 1 million bottles in a year, all hand-blown. There are two additional glass cases, one of which contains a collection of deep cut crystal from the 1890s, and five legendary pieces of colored glass from 1911. There is a special series of colored glass from the 1920s—very representational of the period in deep grey, amethyst and aquamarine. The museum displays a total of 800 pieces. These select pieces were culled from the archives of nearly 16,000 pieces.

Throughout the ages, Norwegians have created a variety of folk arts and crafts. Their work is very traditional, inspired from the elements of nature—some for practical reasons and others for social and cultural expression. Evidence of this fine work still exists today: pelts of reindeer for floor coverings and blankets, looms for weaving sheep wool clothing, and massive sculpture carved from solid blocks of granite and cast bronze. Norwegians are clearly proud of their land and heritage, and one visit to this magnificent country will leave an everlasting impression on how we see the world.

Above: Broken ice caps on a frozen fjord hints spring is near.

Right: Cold winter days have little effect on daily routine in Tromso.

*Above: A group of Norwegian skiers
break for lunch before continuing a day
of cross-country skiing.*

*Right: Many Norwegian skiers enjoy the
adventure and solitude of skiing alone.*

*Following pages 122-123: At 2:30 am
in the month of May, it is still only
dusk in Svolvaer, Lofoten.*

Nancy Kerrigan

24 years old
5 feet, 4 inches
115 pounds
Stoneham, MA

WHEN EVY SCOTVOLD TALKS ABOUT Nancy of the Laughing Eyes, he refers not to the song but to the figure skater he has coached to within one of her long eyelashes of the top of the world. "When she's laughing, she's good," Scotvold says of Nancy Kerrigan.

For Kerrigan, the 13 months beginning January of 1992 were filled with laughter. She finished third in the Olympic Winter Games, second in the World Championships and won her first U.S. national championship.

But as even the most accomplished figure skaters often are reminded, ice is slippery. Entering the freestyle program of the 1993 World Championships with the lead, she stumbled to fifth place in the final standings.

Instead of pouting, Kerrigan went snowmobiling, then returned home to begin sessions with a sports psychologist to assist her in confronting pressure. Now, as she prepares for her second Olympic Winter Games, Scotvold sees a new look in her eyes.

"She's got big fires burning in her," he says.

Underneath the poster girl exterior that last year landed her among People magazine's 50 Most Beautiful People is a gritty athlete who grew up chipping her teeth playing ice hockey with her two brothers.

Still living at home while attending Boston's Emmanuel College, she has solid support from her welder father, Dan, and her mother, Brenda, who is legally blind.

When Nancy is learning a new program, she walks and talks her way through it in the living room so her mother

can grasp it. But Brenda can only watch her daughter skate with the benefit of a TV monitor placed inches from her face.

"Everyone tells me, 'Nancy, she's beautiful'," Brenda says. "When they show a close-up, I say, 'Yeah, she really is."

Oksana Baiul

16 years old
5 feet, 2 1/2 inches
95 pounds
Dnepropetrovsk, Ukraine

WHEN HER NAME IS ANNOUNCED, Oskana Baiul waits…and waits…and waits before skating to the center of the ice to begin her performance.

"I listen to my skates," she says. "When they can start, they go to the start."

They gave her wise counsel in 1993, when she, at 15, went from ingenue to star by becoming figure skating's youngest ladies world champion since Sonja Henie in 1927. Poetically, Baiul will travel to Henie's native country, Norway, as the favorite to win the Olympic gold medal.

Abandoned when she was two by her father, orphaned at 13 when her mother died of ovarian cancer, stranded later that same year when her coach left the Ukraine for a more lucrative position in Canada, her journey has been filled with heartbreak. Usually wide-eyed, giggly and in the company of a teddy bear, she cannot talk of her hardships without dissolving into tears.

But at least her former coach made sure she was in good hands by sending her to Odessa to train with Galina Zmievskaya, whose most famous pupil, Viktor Petrenko, won the men's figure skating gold medal in 1992 at Albertville, France.

Zmievskaya hesitated before accepting the responsibility. Because Baiul has no family, the coach knew that she would not be adding another skater but another daughter.

Petrenko, who is Zmievskaya's son-in-law, persuaded her to extend the family.

"She is only one girl," he said. "How much can she cost?"

Baiul's triumph is amazing to everyone except her. "I don't have to understand how this has happened," she says. "This gift is from God. My goal is just to skate, to show my best so that the judges will like me."

Brian Boitano

30 years old
5 feet, 11 inches
165 pounds
Sunnyvale, Calif.

As soon as the music started, a calm came over Brian Boitano like he had never felt before on the ice. He looked around and saw golden walls, stationed in each of the places where he would perform his most daring triple jumps, giving him a sense of both strength and protection. "It was like a dream," he said years later.

So was the outcome for him that February night in 1988 at Calgary's Saddledome, where Boitano met the Canadian hero, world champion Brian Orser, in front of a pro-Canadian crowd, and won the Olympic gold medal with one of the most inspiring figure skating performances ever.

That enabled Boitano to enter a world accessible only to a chosen few, touring with the beautiful German champion, Katarina Witt, cashing in on his name with lucrative endorsement deals and asserting his increasing superiority over other men in his sport by winning occasional professional competitions.

But that was not enough for Boitano, who waged a campaign within the International Skating Union to allow professionals to compete in the Olympic Games. Four years after his triumph in Calgary, he was again a champion, this time for all the professionals who wanted to come back as the ISU adopted the so-called "Boitano Rule."

"I don't think I had achieved everything I want from skating," he said after announcing his return. "Until I do that, I can't move on. I want to fulfill all the potential I have."

"I don't expect to duplicate Calgary. No, that was so special that I couldn't improve on it. This is just a progression. My whole skating career has been a work in progress. Of course, wouldn't it be wonderful if it did happen for me again like it did in 1988?"

Katarina Witt

28 years old
5 feet, 5 inches
119 pounds
Chemnitz,
Germany

A WRITER FOR SPORTS ILLUSTRATED once described Katarina Witt as "fresh-faced…blue-eyed…ruby-lipped…12-car pileup gorgeous."

It should be noted that she also is one of the greatest figure skaters of all time. A two-time Olympic gold medalist, she decided last winter that, after being out of competition for four years while touring with Brian Boitano, she will attempt to become the first three-time individual champion since Sonja Henie.

Many people within the sport are skeptical about her chances. Although she has continued to mature artistically, her elegance enhanced by her modeling career, it was apparent even when she won her second gold medal in 1988 that she had slipped athletically.

And since she has been gone, judges have begun placing more emphasis on that aspect of the competition. The most skilled women routinely include seven triple jumps in their freestyle programs. Even at her best, Witt never performed more than five.

So, the cynics wondered, was the announcement of her comeback a publicity stunt?

"That's ridiculous," Witt said. "What do I need more publicity for?"

She has a point. Whether she has an innocent meeting with Alberto Tomba, brief encounters with Donald Trump and Boris Becker or a relationship with Richard Dean Anderson of TV's "MacGyver," her activities provide fertile ground for tabloids throughout the world.

If there were any doubt about her seriousness, it should have been erased when she returned to Chemnitz to work with her former coach, Jutta Mueller, who was such a stern taskmaster during their early years together that she searched the trash can in Witt's room for wrappers from forbidden candy bars.

"I'm not saying I'm going for the gold," Witt said. "But I'm going to show the best skating I can. I'm an athlete, and gutsy enough to fight."

Torvill & Dean

Jayne Torvill
36 years old
5 feet, 1 inch
105 pounds
Nottingham,
England

Christopher Dean
35 years old
5 feet, 10 inches
154 pounds
Nottingham,
England

IN HIS BEST-SELLING BIOGRAPHY OF Jayne Torvill and Christopher Dean, author Bernard Ford wrote that seeing them dance together on ice is "like watching God skate."

Ice dancing judges in the 1984 Olympic Winter Games at Sarajevo had no quarrel with that divine assessment. All nine awarded perfect scores of 6.0 to Torvill and Dean for their artistic impression of Ravel's "Bolero." Never before, or since, have skaters

been so unanimously appreciated in the Olympic Games.

Appreciated does not begin to describe the feeling for them in Great Britain, where they shared the distinction as the No. 1 couple with Charles and Diana.

The prince and princess of the middle class, Dean is the son of an electrician, and Torvill is the daughter of a newsstand owner. When they began skating together, he was a policeman, and she was a clerk.

So, it is no wonder that T&D were back on London's front pages last spring, when they announced they are returning to the 1994 Olympic Winter Games.

After a decade of touring as professionals, they have more rapport than ever. "When we're skating together, if her eyelid's in the wrong place, I can feel it," Dean says.

Perhaps one reason for their success is that romance never entered into it. She is married to a man involved in the rock and roll business, and he separated last summer from French ice dancer Isabelle Duchesnay.

"Even though it's a return to something we've done before, it's a new challenge," Torvill says of their decision to compete in Lillehammer. "We still feel like we have a lot to offer to the sport. It's like a new lease on life."

Alberto Tomba

27 years old
6 feet
200 pounds
Bologna, Italy

AS A YOUNG MAN STRUGGLING TO earn a place on Italy's junior ski team, Alberto Tomba was watching a film of Ingemar Stenmark when he asked, "Who is that guy?" Told that Stenmark was considered the greatest slalom skier of all time, Tomba responded, "It doesn't matter. In a few years, I'll be better."

Not only did Tomba eventually turn his boast into fact, he decided that no mortal man was worthy of comparison to him.

"I am the Messiah of skiing," he declared.

In the 1992 Winter Games at Albertville, France, a town he rechristened "Alberto-ville," Tomba became the first man to win giant slalom gold medals in two straight Olympic Games. Considering that he finished second in the 1993 World Cup standings in the event, a three-peat at Lillehammer's Olympic Winter Games is not out of the question. He also has won gold and silver medals in the slalom.

But it is not on the slopes where he has gained his most notoriety. Whether he is mooning a waiter in a Rome restaurant, diving into a swimming pool with a topless model or performing headstands for contestants in the Miss Italy contest, *Tomba la Bomba* is as likely to appear on the front page of his country's newspapers as the sports pages.

"Maybe I'm crazy just a little bit," he concedes.

He is not so crazy, however, that he has allowed "La Dolce Vita," the sweet life, to distract him from his skiing. Before the 1992 Olympic Winter Games, he hired a personal coach, who convinced him to take training and diet more seriously. And during the Miss Italy contest, Tomba began a steady relationship with one of the contestants—the winner, of course.

Does that mean he is ready to settle down?

Perhaps not. Asked last winter if he were ready to set a wedding date, he replied, "February 30."

Julie Parisien

**22 years old
5 feet, 8 inches
150 pounds
Auburn, Maine**

WITH THE FASTEST TIME AFTER THE first of two slalom runs in the 1992 Olympic Winter Games, Julie Parisien appeared destined to win a medal, perhaps even a gold. But on the second run, she went against her nature, as well as the nature of the event, and conservatively skied to a fourth-place finish.

One of the first to console her was her brother, Jean Paul, who told her she could put the disappointment behind her by winning a gold medal in the 1993 World Championships.

Ten months later, one week before Christmas, Jean Paul was killed in an automobile accident in Maine.

As one of the Unites States' best-known skiing families, the Parisiens long ago accepted risks as part of their lives. Besides, Julie, the world's No. 1-ranked slalom skier in 1991-92, younger sister Anna is a member of the U.S. B Team and older brother Robbie competes on the professional circuit.

But Jean Paul's death was senseless, caused after his car was forced off an icy highway and into a thicket of trees when sideswiped by a man who later was charged with drunk driving.

Julie took several weeks off to confront her grief. As a result, she fell to seventh place in the 1992-93 slalom ranking. But she returned to competition in time for a second-place finish in the World Championships.

Recalling her conversation with Jean Paul after the Olympic Games, she had hoped for better.

"I'm skiing not just for myself," she said. "I'm living my life with my brother and for my brother. I'm really happy with my silver medal, but I feel that I have let him down in a way by not getting the gold."

"I know he's up there, saying, 'C'mon, you can do better than that.'"

Perhaps in Lillehammer.

Bonnie Blair

29 years old
5 feet, 5 inches
130 pounds
Champaign, IL

BONNIE BLAIR MIGHT NOT BE A BORN speedskater, but she is close. On the day of her birth in Cornwall, N.Y., her father, Charlie, dropped off her mother at the hospital, then hurried to a speedskating meet to see three of his other five children compete.

He learned that he had a sixth child when Bonnie's arrival was announced over the public address system at the track.

Virtually ever since, she has been making news at speedskating ovals. Arguably the best women's winter athlete the United States has ever produced, she became the first in 1992 to win gold medals in consecutive Olympic Games. She added two to her collection at Albertville, France, in the 500 meters and 1000, complementing her gold in the 500 and bronze in the 1000 from 1988.

"I look at her like some kind of speedskating goddess," says Mary Docter, her U.S. teammate from the last three Olympic Games.

But Blair remains as unaffected as she was as a schoolgirl in Champaign, Illinois, where the Patrolmen's Benevolent Association raised money to support her training. Policemen sold bumper stickers identifying her as their favorite speeder.

As one Midwestern sports columnist wrote, she is "the kid sister of all America…as genuine as a peanut butter and jelly sandwich…unscarred by sophistication." Her biography in the U.S. International Speedskating Association's media guide reveals that she enjoys "softball, golf, writing letters, watching TV and baking cookies."

She was the first woman in more than a decade to challenge the East Germans, who once dominated the sport, but she never considered them rivals. When one of her fiercest competitors, Christa Rothenburger Luding, gave birth in 1991, Blair sent her a baby gift.

Could this be the same woman whose coach, Peter Mueller, describes as "a killer" on the track?

Dan Jansen

28 years old
6 feet
190 pounds
West Allis, WI

THE TELEPHONE IN SPEEDSKATER DAN Jansen's room in the Olympic village at Calgary rang at 6 a.m. It was his brother Mike, calling from a hospital room in Wisconsin, where their 27-year-old sister, Jane, was losing her struggle with leukemia. Mike held the receiver to Jane's ear so that Dan could speak with her one last time.

Three hours later, she was dead.

Persuaded by his family that Jane would have wanted him to skate in the 500 meters later that day, Dan was too distraught to concentrate, and fell. Four days later, he fell again in the 1000 meters.

Jansen did not win a medal in the 1988 Olympic Winter Games at Calgary, but he earned the admiration of a nation. He received more than 10,000 letters, including one from President Reagan. The most precious one, however, came from a Special Olympian from Doylestown, Pennsylvania.

"My father died just before I competed in the 1981 Special Olympics," Mark Arrowhead wrote. "I want to share one of my gold medals with you because I don't like to see you not get one."

In a perfect world, Jansen would have won a medal of his own in the 1992 Olympic Winter Games at Albertville, France to put alongside Mark's inside the glass trophy case in his parents' dining room. He missed by two-tenths of a second, finishing fourth in the 500.

But the story, happily, did not end there. He skated better than ever in 1993, finishing first in the World Cup standings in the 500 and second in the 1000. In the final race of the year, at Calgary, he set the world record in the 500.

And, in May, his wife Robin gave birth to their first child, a girl. They named her Jane.

Toni Nieminen

18 years old
5 feet, 7 inches
128 pounds
Vaaksy, Finland

DISTANCE RUNNER PAAVO NURMI WAS the original Flying Finn, but no Finn has ever flown at such a young age as Toni Nieminen. And, unlike Nurmi, Nieminen literally soared.

In 1992, at age 16, the ski jumper became the youngest man ever to win a gold medal in the Olympic Winter Games with first-place finishes in the big hill and team events. He also won a bronze in the normal hill event.

One of the first jumpers to adopt the innovative V-style, he was anointed "a genius" by famed Austrian coach Toni Innauer.

But, upon his return home from the Olympic Games, Nieminen proved to be all too normal, subject to distractions that would bring almost any teenager crashing back to earth.

As his personal coach, Jurkka Laine, recalls, Nieminen was greeted like a rock star. "It was like a big chaos," Laine

said. "The Finns are crazy about winter sports. There was TV, press, the young girls. It was crazy. Half the fan letters still are not opened."

Then there was Toyota, now the most famous car in Finland. After Nieminen's sponsor rewarded him with a snazzy white Toyota Celica GT4, the Finnish government gave him a driver's license before the legal age of 18 so that he could drive himself to practice. He soon discovered that he liked driving the car more than he did practicing.

Predictably, he went into a tailspin, falling from first place in the overall World Cup standings in 1991-92 to 50th last season. At one point, Finland's national coach, Matti Pulli, unceremoniously dropped him from the team.

Regarding that as a wakeup call, Nieminen, who comes from a family of six in a small village, returned to work, giving Finland its highest finish — fifth on the normal hill — in the 1993 World Championships.

Says Laine," He has paid his dues."

Vegard Ulvang

30 years old
6 feet
165 pounds
Kirkenes, Norway

NORWEGIANS' REVERENCE FOR CROSS country skiing is old as it is deep, beginning during the civil war of 1206 when warriors on skis carried the infant Prince Haakon 33 miles through a blizzard over frozen terrain to escape assassins.

In Vegard Ulvang, Norway has a hero to match its legends.

During the 1992 Olympic Winter Games, he won four cross-country skiing medals, three golds and a silver. His teammate, Bjorn Daehlie, also won three gold medals as Norwegians monopolized their favorite winter sport.

But as renowned as Ulvang has become throughout the world for his skiing, he is equally appreciated in his home country as a daring adventurer. He has skiied across Greenland, where he lost 26 pounds on an icy 15-day trek; canoed 600 miles down a Si-berian river with his Russian cross-country foe and close friend, Vladimar Smirnov; and climbed the highest mountains on five continents, most of them with Arne Ess, husband of singer Diana Ross.

Despite his tenacity in and out of competition, Ulvang dismisses his rugged individualist image, calling it a media invention. He was particularly offended when a TV commentator nicknamed him, "The Terminator."

"I saw the film," Ulvang says. "I didn't like it."

A native of a small town at the mouth of a fjord in northernmost Norway, where, he said, "you can walk for a week without seeing a man," the son of a history teacher studied math and physics at the University of Oslo for three years before departing to become a full-time athlete and explorer.

He might return some day to complete his education, but he emphasizes that he has other mountains to climb, perhaps even Mt. Everest.

"There are many adventures to do still," he said.

But, first, there is the challenge of competing in the Olympic Winter Games in his home country. "I've been getting better every year," he said.

Brian Shimer

**31 years old
5 feet, 11 inches
190 pounds
Naples, Florida**

WHAT IS A FLORIDIAN LIKE BRIAN Shimer doing in a sport like bobsled?

"I like the speed, the crashing," he says. "It's the danger that draws me to the sport."

Shimer has done little crashing of late. Last winter, he was the world's leading driver in combined two-man and four-man standings, a result that humiliated the Europeans, particularly the Germans, who have dominated the sport for the last three decades. After Shimer's victory in a World Cup four-man race at Winterberg, Germany, two members of the German team refused to attend the awards ceremony.

"It may really bother them now that they know we're not a fluke," Shimer says. "We're going to be in contention for a medal at every race."

Including the Olympic Winter Games, in which the United States has not won a bobsled medal since 1956?

"I've got a burning desire inside that I can't stop un-til I achieve the goal that I've set for myself, and that is winning an Olympic medal," he says.

If he does, he will owe some credit to the U.S. coach, Meinhard Nehmer, who, while competing for East Germany, became the only driver to win three Olympic gold medals. Another contributor is auto racer Geoff Bodine, who has been working with Shimer to develop state-of-the-art sleds.

This is not the first time Shimer has turned to another sport for assistance. He finished seventh in the two-man competition in the 1992 Olympic Winter Games with his teammate, pro football running back Herschel Walker.

Shimer himself was a football player at Moorehead State. Two other members of his four-man team last winter were former college football players, and the other had been a track and field sprinter in college.

"We've always had the best athletes in the world," Shimer says. "It's just a matter of coming together as a team."

Alpine Skiing, Giant Slalom

THIS EVENT IS SIMILAR TO THE SLALOM, EXCEPT THE COURSE is longer, the gates are farther apart, and the turns are not as sharp. As a result, the speeds are more dizzying, which some skiers, such as Austria's overall World Cup champion, Anita Wachter, believe places a greater premium on control than the Slalom.

Alpine Skiing Combined

SKIERS RACE AGAINST EACH OTHER ON ONE DOWNHILL RUN one day and on two slalom runs the next day—the two extremes of Alpine Skiing—to determine the best overall skier. It is not wise to bet against Luxembourg's Marc Giradelli, who last season became the only man to win five overall World Cup championships.

Ice Hockey

OLYMPIANS DO NOT PLAY THE GAME THE WAY THE PROS IN the NHL do, which is a blessing for fans who prefer the beauty of the sport to the beast. This game rewards speed, accurate passing and teamwork. Those are the trademarks of Russian players who, under the Soviet flag, have won every gold medal except two since 1956.

Men's Figure Skating

BESIDES ARTISTIC AND TECHNICAL EXCELLENCE, JUDGES LOOK for the power characteristic of four-time world champion Kurt Browning of Canada. But the most important asset for the men might be stamina. Often, the champion is the one who can stay on his feet through the grueling 4 1/2-minute freestyle program.

Nordic Skiing

SKI JUMPERS ARE JUDGED EQUALLY ON DISTANCE AND form. But rarely do the best jumpers, such as Norway's Espen Bredesen, travel far without excellent form. For athletes with a fear of flying, Cross-Country Skiing demands more of them physiologically than any other sport. Provide them with guns and targets, and you have the Biathlon.

Pairs Figure Skating

NOT FOR THE FAINT OF HEART, THE LIFTS, THROWS AND swoops are so daring that they make even the required death spiral seem tame. For the acrobatic elements, the best pairs today, such as Russian Olympic champions Ekaterina Gordeeva and Sergei Grinkov, have male partners large enough to easily hoist and heave the females.

Ladies' Figure Skating

THE THREE E'S TRADITIONALLY ASSOCIATED WITH THIS event are elegance, expression and élan. In recent years, judges have demanded a fourth. Energy. No one has more of that than 1993 world silver medalist Surya Bonaly of France. Whoever best combines all the essentials in her four-minute freestyle program will win gold.

Ice Dancing

SKATERS WITH BALLETIC TRAINING, SUCH AS REIGNING world champions Maia Usova and Alexander Zhulin, are well-suited for an event that requires intricate footwork, coordination and creative flair. Unlike their pairs counterparts, ice dancers are required to remain in close contact and unison as they interpret the music.

Luge

NO WINTER ATHLETES EXPOSE THEMSELVES TO MORE danger than sliders, who ride flat on their backs down a bending track at 70 miles per hour on a four-foot long, 18-inch wide sled with no mechanical steering or braking devices. The United States has never won a Luge medal, but had its first world champion in 1993 with Wendel Suckow.

Bobsled

MAN BEGAN SLEDDING 15,000 YEARS AGO, STRETCHING animal skin between two pieces of wood for transportation. Today, champions such as Switzerland's Gustav Weder hurtle themselves down a mile-long course at speeds up to 90 miles per hour, braking for hairpin curves, in $130,000 state-of-the-art two-man and four-man sleds.

Alpine Skiing, Slalom

THE ULTIMATE TEST OF PRECISION FOR TECHNICAL SKIERS, such as Switzerland's reigning World Cup Champion, Vreni Schneider, the slalom requires them to weave in and out of the blue and red-flagged gates in two runs over different courses. There are between 55 and 75 gates for men and between 40 and 60 for women.

Alpine Skiing Downhill

"THE OLYMPIC FACTBOOK," LICENSED BY THE U.S. Olympic Committee, states the following as fact: "Downhillers are considered by other skiers to be insane." Even if they have the quiet, shy demeanor of Norway's Kjetil Andre Aamodt, they often are reckless on skis, racing down steep courses in a blur at 80 miles an hour.

Alpine Skiing Super Giant Slalom

SEEKING AN EVENT THAT WOULD COMBINE the speed and drama of the Downhill with the more exacting Giant Slalom, Olympic officials added the Super-G to the program in 1988. That gave fearless downhillers, such as France's Carole Merle, another opportunity to compete, albeit one that challenges them with high-speed turns.

Freestyle Skiing

WHEN COMPETITIONS WERE FIRST ORGANIZED IN THE late '60s and early '70s, they were considered for hot-doggers only. But the sport went legit in 1992, when Moguls became on official Winter Olympic event. The United States' Donna Weibrecht was the first women's gold medalist. In 1994, the aerialists will flip for medals.

Speedskating

ATTIRED IN AERODYNAMIC BODYSUITS, THE BEST SPRINTERS race 40 miles per hour, faster than any other humans under their own power. Traditionalists equally value long-track skaters, such as Norway's Johann Olav Koss, who have the endurance for 10,000 meters. For action fans, there is short track, the roller derby on ice.

Author: Robert Wulf
Edited by: Jennifer Rabbitt Hyndman
Design Director: Thomas K. Walker, GRAF/x
Principal Photography: John Connell
Olympic Writer: Randy Harvey, L.A. Times
Director of Special Projects: Lynne Spencer
Creative Assistant: Sarah McNeill
Publication Coordinator: Judy Kammler
Design Assistance: Sherri Whitmarsh, GRAF/x
Publisher: Robert Woolery

Foreign Coordinators:
Norwegian Tourist Board, NY
Mr. Harold Hansen

Norwegian Tourist Board, Oslo
Jorun Aasen

Oslo Promotions
Ms. Peggy Schlytter

Bergen Tourist Board, Bergen
Ms. Liv Hege Tveit

Fagernes Regional Guide
Mr. Svein Erik Skii

Troll Park Manager, Lillehammer
Ms. Ann Irene Saeternes

Stavanger Tourist Association
Inger Munch-Ellingsen

Lofoten Coordinator:
Asbjorn Gabrielsen

Ardal Coordinator:
Oyvind Wang

The West Norway Museum of Applied Arts:
Trond Indahl/ Curator

Official Government Support:

Royal Norwegian Consulate General:
Consul Generals of Norway:
The Honorable Anfin Ullern
The Honorable Janis Bjorn Kanavan
The Honorable John Petter Opdahl
The Honorable Jan Erik Leikvang
The Honorable Dag Mork Ulnes
The Honorable Bjarne Grindem

The Norwegian Embassy:
Norwegian Ambassador:
The Honorable Kjell Vibe

The Royal Ministry of Foreign Affairs

Haug International:
Mr. Arne F. Haug

University Museum of National Antiquities

Orange County Office of Protocol:
Chief of Protocol:
Ms. Gayle M. Anderson

Olympic Organizations:

The United States Olympic Committee:
Mr. Barry King
Ms. Sandra Baldwin

The Atlanta Committee for the Olympic Games
The Atlanta Centennial Olympic Properties:
Mr. William Porter Payne
Dr. Harvey W. Schiller
Mr. R.E. Hollander
Ms. Judy P. Steele
Mr. Doug Lothes
Ms. Alison Davis Dillen

International Olympic Committee:
Michael R. Payne

Lillehammer Olympic Organizing Committee:
Gerhard Heiberg, President
Asmund Berge, Legal
Randi Stordal, Legal
Bjorn Sandnes, Press Spokesman

Lillehammer Olympic Information Center

Accommodations and Travel:
SAS Park Royal Hotel, Oslo
SAS Scandinavian Airlines
Hotel Continental, Oslo
Molla Hotel, Lillehammer
Hammer Home Hotel, Lillehammer
Hotel Park Pension, Bergen
Ullensvang Hotel, Lofthus
Utne Hotel, Utne
Fisherman's Chalet, A
Atlantic Hotel, Stavnager
Klingenberg Hotel

Acknowledgments:
Else and Erik Anfinsen
Hadelands Garden Vestre Gamkinn
Arne Sorlie

Contributing Photography:
Allsports Photography (USA) Inc.
Stephanie Mullen

Page 1.	Pal Hermansen
Page 13.	Espen Bratlie
Page 92.	Pal Hermansen
Page 94-95	Helge Eek
Page 98-A	J.B. Olsen/R. Sorensen
Page 98-99	Pal Hermansen
Page 116	Pal Hermansen
Page 117	J.B. Olsen/ R. Sorensen
Page 118	Pal Hermansen
Page 119	Espen Bratlie
Page 120	Espen Bratlie
Page 121	Pal Hermansen
Page 123	Pal Hermansen
Page 125A	Vandystadt
Page 125B	Mike Powell
Page 126	David Leah
Page 127A	Vandystadt
Page 127B	Chris Cole
Page 129	Vandystadt
Page 130A	Tim Defrisco
Page 130B	Cy White
Page 131	Shaun Botterill
Page 132A	Nathan Bilow
Page 132B	Vandystadt
Page 133	Pascal Rondeau
Page 134	Mike Powell
Page 135A	Vandystadt
Page 135B	Vandystadt
Page 136A	Vandystadt
Page 136B	Vandystadt
Page 137A	Shaun Botterill
Page 137B	Vandystadt
Page 138A	Bob Martin
Page 138B	Vandystadt
Page 139A	Vandystadt
Page 139B	Vandystadt
Page 139C	Vandystadt
Page 140A	Rick Stewart
Page 140B	Pascal Rondeau
Page 140C	I. Tomlinson
Page 141A	Vandystadt
Page 141B	Simon Bruty
Page 141C	Vandystadt
Page 142A	Rick Stewart
Page 142B	Vandystadt
Page 143A	Cor Mooy
Page 143B	Shaun Botterill

Special Thanks:
Leslie
Danielle
Katie
Samantha
Bob & Barbara
C.J. & Annie
Marie Piscopo
Tom Scott
Tom & Holly
Olivia
David L. Werline
Maureen Ambrose
Sports Illustrated:
Judith B. Bass

Published By:
Milestone Publishing
2805 Catherine Way
Irvine, CA. 92705
714-261-6445

Color Separations:
Bowne Imaging Network
Irvine,CA.

Printer:
Bowne Imaging Network
Irvine, CA.

E-6 Film Processing:
MPS Photo Lab
Fountain Valley, CA.
Hosmer McKoon

Fuji Photo Film Co., Ltd.

Canon U.S.A., Inc.